AF482456

PRISM OF LIFE

A Collection of 100+ Poetry Forms

by

Jeffrey Dacanay Cejero

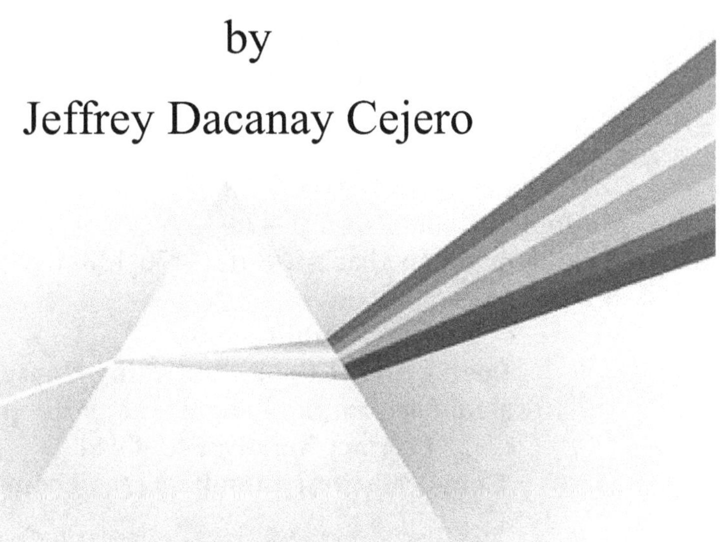

COPYRIGHT © 2021 PRISM OF LIFE: A Collection of 100+ Poetry Forms By Jeffrey Dacanay Cejero

All rights reserved. No part of this publication may be reproduced, distributed, or transmitted in any form or any means, including photocopying, recording, or other electronic or mechanical methods without the prior permission of the publisher and author, except in the case of brief quotations embodied in critical reviews and certain other commercial uses permitted by copyright law may be reproduced or used in any manner without the prior written permission of the copyright owner and publisher.

Edited by Maritess A. Cejero
Illustrations by Jema Elizabeth A. Cejero

Hardbound-978-621-470-136-0
Mobile/Kindle-978-621-470-137-7
Softbound/Paperback-978-621-470-138-4

Published by:
Poetry Planet Book Publishing House
Rosario, Pozorrubio, Pangasinan, Philippines
Contact No.: 09554960044
Email: maritesritumalta@gmail.com

DEDICATION

To my wife, Maritess who always believes in my capabilities and for pushing me to finish this book;

To our three wonderful children, Jema Elizabeth, Mark Wissam, and Catherine Anne who are the source of our inspiration;

To my parents, Mr. Arsenio and Felicitas Cejero, who loved me unconditionally;

To my siblings- Ana Fe, Digna, Estelita, Francis, Nilo, and Junjun and our other relatives who always show support in all my endeavors;

To my family-in-law, the Abellera family who welcomed and considered me as part of their big clan;

To my friends and colleagues who are always there for me; and

To all the poem lovers out there…

This book is dedicated to all of you.

INTRODUCTION

Poetry is a form of literature with the purpose to share ideas, tell stories or express emotions through the use of words that are carefully selected and artistically arranged. It has different forms and each form is as exciting as the other poetry forms. Composing poems using poetry forms helps the poet to touch any idea, emotion, story, or imagery. Reading books with varied poetry forms ensures the readers that they are reading rich and diverse themes.

Life is like a prism. A prism splits white light into seven colors. Each color is equally beautiful and has its distinct characteristics. It symbolizes something and sometimes it affects our emotions or our thinking. Like a prism, life is colorful. It is not only made of happiness and sweetness but sometimes sadness and bitterness.

This poetry book, "Prism of Life: A Collection of 100+ Poetry Forms" shows various examples of poems written in different forms. Poetry forms can either be traditional or invented. Some of the traditional poetry forms included in this book are free verse, sonnet, and haiku while invented poetry forms are blitz, Fibonacci, and monotetra.

This book acts like a prism where light is poetry and poetry forms are the colors in spectrum.

The Author

FOREWORD

It is my pride and honor to introduce you, Jeffrey D. Cejero. I recently met this young upcoming poet on Poetry Planet. His heart and soul beckoned mine from the beginning. With a warm and gentle outlook on life that you can see reflected in his poetry as he enjoys trying many different classes and styles, his poetry is serenely soothing. A gentle waterfall on the soul casting a myriad of prismatic rainbow reflections to engage the mind and spirit. I know that you will enjoy his artful creations as much as I have. Jeffrey lives with his beautiful wife and family in the Philippines. You can meet him in his persona as one of Poetry Planet's dedicated mediators and contributors on Facebook. Enjoy!

Pamela Tennant
USA

ACKNOWLEDGEMENTS

I never dreamed that someday I will be able to make my own book. This book was made possible because of the people close to my heart:

To my wife, Maritess who has always been supportive in my poetry journey. She is the first critic of all my compositions.

To my three children who were always excited to read or listen to every new composition that I make. Their excitement gave me the energy to continue finishing this book. Special mention is given to my eldest, Jema Elizabeth for being the illustrator of this book.

To my entire family and relatives, I am so grateful for having you all in my life.

To Poetry Planet and its founder Ms. Marites Ritumalta, for all the learning experiences I gained from the group. This group trained and sharpened my composition ability, especially on the different poetry forms. It is such an honor to be appointed as one of the moderators of this group with more than 52,000 members.

To my co-moderators in Poetry Planet, Mr. Elmer Gamulo and Ms. Pamela Tennant, who were very responsive to the poetry challenges I posted in the group and for giving suggestions on how to improve my works.

To all the people of Poetry Planet who continue to support and believe in me.

To Filipino Poets in Blossoms, Founder Helen Sarita, and members for all the learning and friendship I gained from the group.

To Mr. Yesu Ben, Ms. Leah Dancel, and Ms. Vee Barnes, for all your posted masterpieces. You are the *Big Three* who I look up to in poetry.

To Ms. Susan Belen, my teacher in poetry, for sharing her techniques in writing and for all her guidance as I took this poetry journey.

To my friend, Rhodora Garcia-Medina for giving her honest opinion on my works.

To all my friends especially in the poetry group, thank you for all the motivation.

And most of all, to our God who is the source of wisdom for bestowing me the skill in weaving words to compose poems and for all the blessings He continuously gives me and my family.

PREFACE

From a single ray of white light, a prism can produce a rainbow of colors. A prism itself is actually crystal clear, but it can produce a kaleidoscope of colors. Life, on the other hand, already has multiple dimensions: sorrow and happiness, failure and success. All of these dimensions can help create or shape a better version of you, but only if you know how to use them to your advantage. You are like a precious crystal-clear diamond, yet you can burst into a rainbow of colors when you allow light to shine on you.

Free verse can create emotionally charged poetry because it can express words the way you want it to and not be constrained about things such as syllable counts, meters, rhymes, and flow. Writing your emotions with formats to follow is a difficult task, but the author managed to write 115 poems with forms. He meticulously studied each format in order to produce poems of exceptional quality. Each poem is thoroughly examined in terms of metrics and syllable count. Being reviewed by experts, he finally finished this amazing book after a year. This poetry collection is appropriate for aspiring writers who want to study and learn more about poetry and its forms.

This book is titled "PRISM OF LIFE" because it is a mash-up of various themes that blend with the writer's emotions. With the help of his family, who created the illustrations and did the editions, this is unquestionably a must-read book for everyone.

The Publisher

TABLE OF CONTENTS

RHYTHM OF JOY
(Abstract Poetry)

Sea and sky, the song of why
Four kids tapping the seabed
Vibrating the cascading bubbles
Giggling, rippling, creating ripples

Crystal wonderful waves are waving
With its musical rolling, swoosh!
Gentle wind melodiously sings
Caressing every creature

Kids dance the rhythm of joy
Burble, splash, joining the fun
Sun smiles and shines so bright,
Shares its light in this joyful sight

KINDNESS
(acrostic)

K- indle the light of humanity
I- gnite your heart of true love
N- urture yourself with gentleness
D-o good things to all the people
N-oble acts still exist in this world
E-xpress love through good deeds
S-erving others is like serving God
S-how love and care to everyone

POINT OF CESSATION
(Ae Freislighe)

In this point of cessation
I fall on you, magnetic
That clears out my negation
Removes the sad cosmetic.

I feel so much elation
Possessing strong kinetic
Happiness and sedation
Making me energetic.

You complete the equation
As if it was prophetic
In this world of creation
You are the best aesthetic.

I feel your strong sensation
You were like an athletic
In my active mentation
In this point of cessation.

Illustrated by: Jema Elizabeth A. Cejero

THE VOYAGE
(Alphabet Poetry)

A paper boat looks mighty.
Breeze whispering the shorty,
Chanting songs with clarity,
Dancing the waves that's salty,
Expressing love and beauty,
Finding its dreams in misty.
Gentle waves, sweet and flirty,
Humming a little ditty.
In this voyage, it's worthy.
Joy is the totality.
Knowing its capacity
Like stars of eternity
Must sail though it looks pity.
Navigate with Almighty.
Only opportunity,
Paper boat can be nifty.

Quest is its mentality,
Raging waves are all dusty.
Sail, face life adversity
Towards progressivity.
Unlock your ability.
Vast sea is for liberty.
With waves of tranquility,
Xeric, great vitality.
You live in prosperity
Zeal for solidarity.

ACTS OF NATURE
(Amphion)

Nature is angels of music,
Fairies of looks,
And owls in brooks.
Its kisses are cure like magic.
Pains of the past,
Sorrowful blast
Can simply be healed by nature.
Sunshine flowers,
Meteor showers
Are kind acts of nature so pure.

MASTERPIECES
(Anagrammatic Poetry)

Space spits Mars.
Master traps mass.

Par is a star.
It acts spar.

Mist pierces mares.
Masters care hares.

Rats sip ice creams.
Pests create teams.

Map stamps pass.
Mice stir crass.

Pears are tears.
Priest crests spears.

Spices, cases,
I see pieces.

CHOOSING THE RIGHT WORDS
(Ars Poetica Poetry)

A poem is a rainbow painted in the sky
With its colorful smile hanging up high.

Like fire, a poem is warm and shining,
Like fireflies glowing in the evening.

A poem is made from thousands of bees,
Sweetest words of honey buzzing in trees.

Its words are fragrant like flowers
Where birds cascading in showers.
....
A poem connects all the spaces
Unifying the universe in all places.

It has the power traversing time
Connecting any point in rhyme.

A poem is composed of twinkling stars,
As mysterious as the glorious red Mars.

Its words are powerful like the Big Bang
While the black hole fang starts to clang.
....
Like seasons, a poem should make you wonder
Whizzing autumn, winter, spring and summer.

A poem must be everyone's chocolate.
Dripping, dropping, drinking in a faucet.

A poem is cure for a heart in pain
That even science can't explain.

To write a poem, always use the right words.
It's a golden rule in all poetry worlds.

TRUE HAPPINESS
(Awdl Gywydd Poetry)

My love, thanks for everything.
Under this wing of true love,
We are brought to reach the sky.
We flew so high, clouds above.

In this celestial glory,
Our love story has begun.
You and I facing this space.
The divine grace blest us one.

I have nothing more to ask.
I'll do the task to serve you.
You are the moon of my life.
Please be my wife, this is true.

Having you is my sole dream.
You're like a stream of blessings,
Full of love and compassion.
You're a fashion of love wings.

My love, I'm so much grateful.
My life is full of sweetness.
This is all because of you.
I witnessed true happiness.

NEVER BEEN MINE
(Ballad Poetry)

Standing alone in her absence
Memories lingering in this vast,
I could clearly sense her presence
And started thinking back of the past.

Crystal teardrops washed my sad sooth.
Her clear voice was as sweet as honey.
Hearing her lies as if the truth.
Her love words had always been fancy.

First love, was this my fate with her?
Is first love, a love that never dies?
How long shall I endure, suffer?
My first love, please let me free and rise.

I still love you but I regret
This feeling, deception, your false heart.
Hoping I could truly forget.
Love that was never mine from the start.

MEMORIES OF THE PAST
(Ballade Poetry)

I looked up the sky and I felt so gay
As our memories are being unfold.
This place is the witness of yesterday.
You are the true gem that glistens like gold.
You're the warmth, the gentle fire in this cold.
You're the beautiful flower in this vast.
How I wish you were mine till we get old.
The treasured day, memories of the past.

Beautiful smiles are on my face today
As rainbow appears, a sight to behold.
Waiting for you, my true love in this bay.
Your unbreakable oath, that's what I hold.
You're the flower of gold, my marigold.
How I wish my love, memories would last,
If destiny could only be controlled.
The treasured day, memories of the past.

Breeze whistled and fairies came out to play.
Cicadas chanted, love story was told.
The setting sun smiled and showed me the way.
Towering trees swayed and gentle waves rolled.
The birds were singing and I was consoled.
The nature cheered me up and made a blast.
How I really wish, time would be unrolled.
The treasured day, memories of the past.

You're the sweetest memory to uphold.
You gave me true love, no one can't surpass.
This is our love story being untold.
The treasured day, memories of the past.

IF YOU STILL DARE
(Barzeletta Poetry)

The moon smiling so bright, shining the land.
The stars glowing in band, twinkling tonight.
Cool breeze gently kissed me, soothing my soul.
Playmates of the big roll, no one can see.
Swaying, dancing branches, movement so strong.
Fairies who came along, beauty glances.
Seeing glowing fireflies in gold flickers.
Hearing their sweet bickers, nothing but lies.
Nature is your best friend, take it with care.
If you still dare, prepare your ass to bend.

THE DARKEST NIGHT
(Blank Verse Poetry)

Have you ever wondered or asked yourself
When will be the moment for you to shine?
Look at those stars, shining, twinkling tonight.
During daytime, these stars seem not around.
The truth, they are always up in the sky.
They are being prepared by this bright sun.
They are under the care of their mother,
Training her kids how to face a dark night.
When their mother started to set them free,
These stars are not afraid facing the night.
They view the darkest night as a bright chance
Each star trying to shine, showing its light.
They don't compete, instead they give support
With each other and shine in harmony.
I know you are a star, don't be afraid
To be covered by the dark wings of night.
Believe and trust yourself, your night has come.
Embrace this night, it's time for you to shine.
And remember, shine with the other stars.
It's the best way to beat this darkest night.

FIRE IN WINTER
(Blitz)

Stars are bright
Stars are fire
Fire your love
Fire of life
Life is joy
Life is sweet
Sweet success
Sweet is you
You are my love
You are the moon
Moon is smiling
Moon is shining
Shining day
Shining heart
Heart of joy
Heart of gold
Gold is precious
Gold is rare
Rare lady
Rare gem
Gem sparkles
Gem of future
Future flower
Future honey
Honey is sweet
Honey is lasting
Lasting seasons
Lasting partner
Partner kisses

Partner hugs
Hugs of support
Hugs are warmth
Warmth in winter
Warmth of the sun
Sun golden rays
Sun sings songs
Songs fill me up
Songs of morning
Morning prayer
Morning dew
Dew on grasses
Dew in spring
Spring blossoms
Spring and summer
Summer gentle touch
Summer and winter
Winter arrives
Winter snow
Snow
Arrives

FRIENDS
(Bob and Wheel Poetry)

True friends
are extremely rare.
When problem descends,
They truly show care
And love that defends.

The fakes,
Abundant as sands,
Treacherous as snakes,
Have unhelping hands
And count your mistakes.

THE SEEDS
(The Bop Poetry)

Flowers are the angels sent down by heaven.
They give happiness and inspiration to everyone.
Truly, they are wonderful gifts to mankind.
So one day, I decided to have my own garden,
To give colors and fragrance to my dull surroundings,
To attract butterflies as my company in this lonely place.

I love flowers but flowers don't love me.

I visited the garden of my friendly neighbor.
Hers is really a sanctuary of angels in rainbow colors,
Emitting the sweetest scent that attracted my soul.
She taught me how to take care of these angels.
She even gave me free seeds for me to plant.
I also visited flower shops to buy some seeds.
I want angels that would shock the whole world.
Planted these seeds and gave some to my neighbor.

I love flowers but flowers don't love me.

Every morning, I visited my garden full of hope and smiles,
Expecting the seeds have started its germination.
Weeks have already passed but none have grown.
My neighbor visited me and checked my garden.
She told me a shocking revelation
That the seeds I gave her last month were all bad seeds!

I love flowers but flowers don't love me.

BRIDGE TO HEAVEN
(Breccbairdne Poetry)

Flowers flow freely
Shooting sprouting showers.
Bright beautiful pigments
Fiddling the fenced flowers.

Fairies fly flashing
Fleeting friendly cherries.
Sweet-scent, red ripe berry
Attracting the fairies.

Heaven has opened.
Garden guarding haven
Protecting a rainbow,
The bright bridge to heaven.

A METAPHOR OF SHARP KNIVES
(Bref Double Poetry)

Life is indeed a metaphor.
Every happening in our lives,
Our feelings, the deep wounds we have,
All can be linked to this device.
Watching the sharp waves on the shore
As the cold heavy rain arrives.
It reminds us that a calm life
Is not always in paradise.
We have always to be ready.
Prepare what the future derives.
It might be dull or happy life.
Life is a knife cutting a spice.
Life on this land, have to explore.
Life, a metaphor of sharp knives.

BABIES
(Byr A Thoddaid Poetry)

In a home, babies are flowers.
Their scents are heavenly showers
Making the home a place of happiness.
Happy hearts hive this nest.

In a home, babies are angels.
Their voices are music that dwells
Making all members in the family,
Feel fullness in dilly.

In a home, babies are God's gift.
With problems, they give us a lift.
They are the best source of inspiration,
Instill aspiration.

COMPASSION
(Casbairdne Poetry)

This dear world needs empathy.
Clear, true word of companion
Brings joy which is important
With rich wings called compassion.

SEASONS OF LOVE
(Cascade Poetry)

Summer is showers of love in sunshine.
Autumn is epitome of love in red and gold.
Winter is glitters of love in a cold night.
Spring is wings of love that bring hope.

The sun shouts its radiance, shining the lands.
Birds are singing, flowers and trees are swaying.
Two hearts meet and bath in warm love.
Summer is showers of love in sunshine.

The sun begins to get colder, days are becoming shorter.
Sunset glows in spectacular hues, every leaf is a flower.
Two hearts madly in love, enjoying the vivid sight.
Autumn is epitome of love in red and gold.

Then the sun gives the shortest day, snow is everywhere.
The once warm love starts to get cold and bare.
Two hearts in love undergoing life challenges.
Winter is glitters of love in a cold night.

But the sun persists to shine, snow starts to melt.
Plants and grasses are showing life, animals are felt.
Two hearts deeply in love rising from the fall.
Spring is wings of love that bring hope.

Illustrated by: Jema Elizabeth A. Cejero

TINY SEED
(Catena Rondo Poetry)

A tiny seed was blown away,
Breeze gently guided the seed.
Landed on barren land in bleed,
A tiny seed was blown away.

Breeze gently guided the seed.
Putting the seed on a barren land,
Scorching heat in the desert sand,
Breeze gently guided the seed.

Putting the seed on a barren land,
Rain came, allowing life to sprout
Leaves grew, bathed in sunshine of spout,
Putting the seed on a barren land.

Rain came, allowing life to sprout.
Years passed, the tiny seed became a tree.
Had flowers and fruits, life was glee and free.
Rain came, allowing life to sprout.

Years passed, the tiny seed became a tree.
Bore fruits, new seeds were born.
It is the hope of the smiling morn.
Years passed, the tiny seed became a tree.

Bore fruits, new seeds were born.
A tiny seed was blown away.
To find its life in a new way.
Bore fruits, new seeds were born.

A tiny seed was blown away,
Breeze gently guided the seed.
Landed on barren land in bleed,
A tiny seed was blown away.

SHINE AT NIGHT
(Cento Poetry)

Just like moons and like suns, (Angelou)
I wandered lonely as a cloud. (Wordsworth)
Between the woods and frozen lake, (Frost)
My heart moves from cold to fire. (Neruda)
Sometime too hot the eye of heaven shines,
(Shakespeare)
And I watered it in fears. (Blake)
Life is a broken-winged bird (Hughes)
That perches in the soul. (Dickinson)
I am the master of my fate. (Henley)
I am the soft stars that shine at night. (Frye)

Sources
Maya Angelou, "Still I Rise"
William Wordsworth, "I Wandered Lonely As A
Cloud"
Robert Frost, "Stopping by Woods On A Snowy
Evening"
Pablo Neruda, "I Do Not Love You Except Because
I Love You"
William Shakespeare, "Shall I Compare Thee To A
Summer's Day"
William Blake, "A Poison Tree"
Langston Hughes, "Dreams"
Emily Dickinson, "Hope Is The Thing With
Feathers"
William Ernest Henley, "Invictus"
Mary Elizabeth Frye, "Do Not Stand At My Grave
And Weep"

LIFE TRUE SENSE
(Cethramtu Rannaigechta Moire Poetry)

It takes night
To see stars.
Glows with love,
Heal our scars.

It takes rain,
And sunlight
For rainbows
To shine bright.

It takes years
For a seed
To grow big
Not to bleed.

As you see
Time, patience
Help you see
Life true sense.

HAPPINESS
(Chanso Poetry)

Happiness is learning to kiss
The bitter pain of perfect bliss
Not to amiss the joy you gain
From any stain that you obtain.

True happiness in any nest
Brings joy and smile in loneliness.
Times of sadness just for awhile
Is a trial from a far mile.

When one's heart sings, he has the wings
To reach the star, to bath in springs,
To strum the strings of a guitar,
Healing the scar of any war.

Happy are those, holding the rose
Of smiling morn and melting snows.
Happiness grows when light is born,
Easing the thorn of any mourn.

IN SEARCH OF MEANING
(Chant Royal Poetry)

Life is a precious gift from Almighty.
Worth is beyond a treasure chest of gold.
Treasure every moment, life is worthy.
Be happy and let the people behold
Your worth that only God could truly know.
Your life is priceless. It should go and grow.
Make your life meaningful and make each chance,
Each opportunity, smile in radiance.
Life is a gift. Helping, serving, loving
And sharing have true passionate fragrance.
Life is a journey in search of meaning.

Life is always a rainbow of beauty.
Hanging in the sky, a smile to behold.
Smiling just after the clouds of misty
Is flourishing flower of marigold.
A smile of red, blue, orange, green, yellow
Including violet and indigo
Wearing all the colors of elegance.
Always wear your smile. Break any hindrance.
Life should always be full of cherishing
To make our existence shine in brilliance.
Life is a journey in search of meaning.

Life grows like trees against adversity.
Challenge the rain even if it is cold.
A small seed in a land of poverty
Growing courageously and should be bold.
Drought, rain or any storm, the seed should grow.

Extreme heat of summer, storm brought by snow
Any adversity, life should advance.
Grow tall, sway with the raging wind and dance.
And time comes, sweet flowers are flourishing.
Fruits of success produced in abundance.
Life is a journey in search of meaning.

Life, a journey of opportunity
We should be like birds, free and not to hold.
Travel and see the whole world in beauty.
The mystery of life, try to unfold.
Go with the wind, ride on the wave and flow.
You can move like a turtle which is slow
But you can be a lightning with fast stance.
Please do not forget to give assistance
To the people by helping and caring.
Life should be like this, live with elegance.
Life is a journey in search of meaning.

Life is fire shining in eternity.
Shine in the dark and give warmth in the cold.
Burn pride but always show humility.
Serve the people, power should be controlled.
Be grateful, be friendly and say hello.
Do good every day. Kindness makes you glow.
Don't hesitate to love. It's a good chance.
Burn life with love to show its full radiance.
Practicing these, life will be promising.
Life is fire, shine the world with your brilliance.
Life is a journey in search of meaning.

Life, a gift from God as a given chance
Just like a tree, life grows in abundance.
Wear rainbows whose smile is so refreshing.
Life is fire that should be burned in radiance.
Life is a journey in search of meaning.

SMILE
(Cinquain Poetry)

The sun
Is still shining
Despite being covered
Of storm clouds shrouding the ground down.
Just smile!

HUGGING A KITTY
(Clerihew Poetry)

Jeffrey Dacanay Cejero,
A macho and a hero, girlfriend is zero.
He's a crying baby at the age of ninety.
He's shaky and sweaty to hug a kitty.

MORNING SUN
(Compound Word Verse Poetry)

The sweet-scent of morning has come
Kissing the land with its hum
Of sunrise.

Life filled the land to start the day.
The bright sun smiled bringing the ray
Of sunlight.

My heart is dancing and singing
For this morning is the joy spring
Of sunshine.

This morning is set to arrange
And make big steps for the great change
Of sunbow.

I prayed and looked up to the sky
To give thank for this morn is my
Sunflower.

STILL BEAUTIFUL
(Constanza Poetry)

Loving you is not a regret.
It's my happiest love story.
Thank you for your sweet memory.

I know that pain is what I get
Once I decided to love you.
My heart is just for you, it's true.

This goodbye, departure is set.
A break up that will come one day.
Still grateful as you go away.

My love for you, hard to forget.
You are the beating of my heart.
You're the sweet smile in every art.

Just like this flowery sunset,
Our ending is still beautiful
For you made my life colorful.

****

Loving you is not a regret.
I know that pain is what I get
This goodbye, departure is set.
My love for you, hard to forget
Just like this flowery sunset.

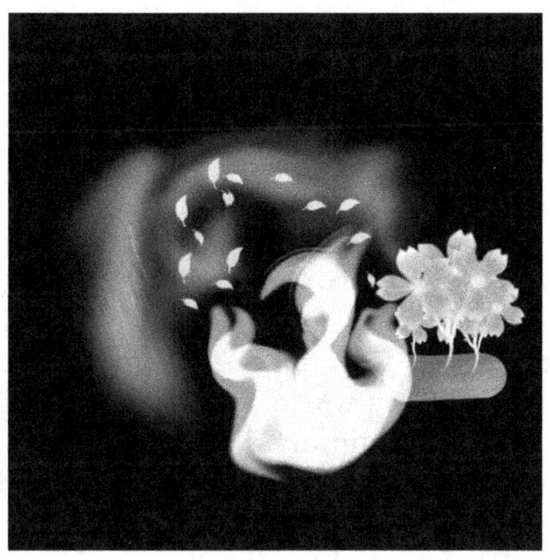

NATURE
(Con-Verse Poetry)

Earth is life-sprouting flowers,
Hues of blessings in showers.

Water is life that cleanse the soul.
Follow its flow to reach the goal.

Air is life, kiss and hug of nature.
Befriend breeze for a better future.

Fire is life, burning love as its fuel.
Triumph every flame, face any duel.

Be one with nature, shield it from any strife.
Take inspiration from nature full of life.

I LOVE YOU
(Curtal Sonnet)

The day I met you, my heart sang in glee.
It was the day my world was bathed in light.
A rainbow smiled and my dark sky turned blue.
The storm was gone, a gentle breeze kissed me.
My old night was no longer cold and tight.
Sweet flowers of love in all colors grew.
Lucky I am for I have now your love.
My lonely life became full of delight.
You're the song of my life and this is true.
These words are for you, my heart is a dove.
I love you.

CHOCOLATE
(Cyrch A Chwta Poetry)

This chocolate is so sweet.
Life feels great, morning to greet
For my heart to sing and beat.
The love I feel is concrete.
Nothing to ask, it's complete
That can make the birds to tweet.
You're the chocolate, my love.
Gift from above, the best treat.

HOPE
(Cywydd Llosgyrnog Poetry)

Hope, the wings in reaching our star
Bringing us to places afar.
Storms of trials are nothing
In achieving set by Supreme.
Let these wings conquer any scheme.
Let this dream make our hearts sing.
Hope, the eyes that could see beyond.
The last wish hidden in a wand.
Strong bond to keep advancing
Towards the land of happiness,
The way in achieving greatness,
See the richness of hoping.
Hope, the promise spring in winter
Where everywhere is sharp splinter
And the center of the storm
Is fast approaching in our place
Destroying, leaving no trace.
Still, grace helps us to reform.
Hope, the only thing that is left.
Everything, taken by a theft.
In a cleft, we're left alone
Trying to face this life challenge.
We smiled even we're hurt, it's strange
Face to change, call of unknown.

HOLDS THE FUTURE
(Daisy Chain Poetry)

Earth is a big living treasure chest.
Chest of gems and chest of happiness.
Happiness is in a meteor shower.
Shower of joy when there is rain.
Rain is hope and life to the land.
Land is a gift that we need to care.
Care our waters, lands and all habitats.
Habitats where wildlife lives in peace.
Peace, live in peace with nature.
Nature is a gift that we need to grow.
Grow like a seed that makes miracles.
Miracles for sharing its blessings.
Blessings like fresh air, shade and fruits.
Fruits of Earth are happiness and life.
Life, use it to take care our wildlife.
Wildlife and habitats are our treasures.
Treasures that are found in all places.
Places like ponds, grasslands and seas.
Seas and habitats are living treasures.
Treasures that might die due to garbage.
Garbage is pollution, kills everyone.
Everyone should be kind to our home.
Home is the best gift we could give.
Give our children this treasure chest.
Chest that has life, holds the future- Earth!

LOVELY NIGHT
(Dansa Poetry)

Starry night, lovely night
Light my site, be my stars.
Heal my wounds, heal my scars.
Be my might, hold me tight
Starry night, lovely night.

With you, we'll win the spars.
Happiness filled our jars.
No more fight, life is bright
Starry night, lovely night.

In my sight, dreams not far
Bright nights are like gold bars.
You're my stars, my night-light
Starry night, lovely night.

DON'T GIVE UP
(Decasyllabic Quatrain Poetry)

Fly higher against the current of wind.
Soar like an eagle, piercing the black clouds.
Flap harder the wings of hope, to ascend
Beating the devils, angels singing loud.

Sail further against the sea raging waves.
Surf these surges, bringing closer to goal.
Beacon of hope, shining along your pave
Towards a dream that makes you full and whole.

Dig deeper against a mountain of rocks.
Never surrender no matter how hard.
Digging is tiring but still break those blocks.
Golds are deep down, along your paths are shards.

Life is not easy and you need to fight.
Cry, let your tears fill up your empty cup.
Endure your darkest night, look for the light.
Success is for those who never give up.

LOVE SHOWER
(Decima Poetry)

In my life, you are my summer.
That gives warmth during my winter.
My days are becoming sweeter.
You are my lover, my flower.
God grants us with this love shower.
My heart is smiling and singing.
Angels and fairies are swinging.
The sun, moon and stars are glancing.
Then the entire world is dancing.

SUMMER
(Deibide Baise Fri Toin Poetry)

It's summer.
My heart beats like a drummer.
Birds and animals sing,
Swing.

This mountain,
Sunshine is like a fountain,
Flows like water in the stream,
Dream.

My flower,
You're my summer and power.
You lighted and warmed my way,
Day.

SUN AND MOON
(Diamante Poetry)

Sun
bright, golden
opening, hoping, shining
day, warmness, night, coolness
closing, dreaming, glowing
lustrous, silvery
moon

SMILING GRACE
(Diminishing Verse Poetry)

Life is a bright smiling grace
Of colors and never a race.
So, enjoy life and reap the ace.

Life is not always white and flawless.
It gives shining wisdom to lawless
And motivating wonders to awless.

Life is seeds that keep growing.
Follow the flow, keep on rowing,
And not to surrender and owing.

And when death wanted to scold
To show that life is dark and cold.
Still, life can laugh even if it's old.

BUTTERFLY EFFECT
(Dizain Poetry)

There was a butterfly that flapped its wings
That blew away the storm, the sun smiled bright.
Changes in the world are brought by small things.
Your little acts of kindness are true light
To someone whose life afraid to make fight.
Kindness grows as it's passed turning into
Hopes and dreams until it turns to be true.
Small acts reverberate in the future
So always do kindness, makes the sky blue.
For a butterfly, its kindness is pure.

CITY LIFE
(Dodoitsu Poetry)

Drinking water is not free.
Noise is the daily music.
Space is always congested.
City life, your dream.

LOVE AND DOVE
(Double Dactyl Poetry)

Butterfly, dragonfly
Colorful, mystical
Here, this wide wilderness
Everyone's love

Marigold, Lavender
Beautiful scenery
Flowery surroundings
Attracting dove

WON'T SURRENDER
(Double Tetractys Poetry)

Failed
Broken
Defeated
Devastated
From these, I'll build the ladder of success.
Failures teach me lessons; life must go on.
Won't surrender
Until I
Have my
Dream!

LIKE A RIVER
(Droigneach Poetry)

Flow like a river that glows forever.
Follow a pathway, big rocks underway.
Plan not to quiver, dreams to deliver.
Courage to display, pebbles underplay.

Be like a river that ne'er surrender.
Flow and meet its foe, time to overthrow.
Persistent ever, now and whenever.
Dream aglow, seas and oceans overflow.

GO

(Echo Verse Poetry)

How I wish you were not away,
Stay!
You're my everything given by Above,
Love.
Without you in my life,
Strife!
To let you go,
No!
Without you, life is meaningless,
Less
Life will never be enough,
Tough.
And will never be the same,
Lame.
But still, thank you,
Go!

THE DOLL OF AN ANGEL
(Elegy)

It's been two years since my home
Made silence as voice of deafening.
Black butterflies were free to roam
And birds of requiem were singing.

In this home, flowers and leaves were tears
And day was the same to a night that lasts.
Today, I entered again this home after two years
And saw a doll, sadness started to blast.

This doll, I tried to ignore by closing my eyes
But my heart was longing to touch it again.
I opened my eyes and sadness began to rise
For golden memories were rushing back then.

I picked up the doll from the dusty floor
Carefully removed the dust that sticked on it.
Each stroke of my hand hit my core
Making my heart to shatter bit by bit.

I started carrying the doll with so much care.
Every second brought a mixture of emotions.
I sang a lullaby that I didn't sing for two years.
My past came back as tears blurred my vision.

You hold the biggest place in my heart.
Your memories are gifts that helped me see
The bigger picture of life and helped me to start.
This doll will no longer be alone for she has me.

HOW I WISH
(Etheree Poetry)

Earth
acts like
a big tree
with so many
birds living in it.
How I wish men were like
Birds, harmless to the big tree.
They sing the songs of care and love
Protecting the tree from pests or worms.
And in return, the tree gives all their needs.

WHEN ANGEL ASCENDS TO HEAVEN
(Eulogy)

Our hearts bled and shattered to pieces.
Unimaginable pain invaded our totality.
Sadness painfully covered our surroundings.
The sun and the moon refused to shine
While all the stars flickered in sadness.
Rainbows turned black and gray in colors
While dark chaotic clouds continued to cry.
We hope and pray somehow, somewhere
Birds would not stop singing the songs of joy,
Rivers and streams would continue to flow
And gentle breeze would whisper to us
Your gentle voice full of love and compassion.
The way you spoke was music to our ears.
Your kindness was contagious, worthy of praise.
For every kid, you were a friend and angel.
For our neighbors, you were their best friend
For having ears that were always ready to listen.
Your fire brought warmth love in our family.
You kept on shining and served as our guide.
Your magnificent colors brightened our lives.
You were very strong, never shown weakness
Fought death for two years with so much courage.
And it is us who were really afraid of losing you.
We forgot that the more we keep you in our midst,
The more we are keeping you from agony.
You showed too much love for our family.
Thank you for all the love and care you gave.
Thank you for all the memories you gifted us.
At this moment, we admit there is too much pain

Because we will not be able to see you again
But don't worry, we'll do our best to accept
That we have to let you go and need to rest.
No wonder, clouds cried when you went away
The sun and the moon refused to shine
While all stars flickered in sadness
And rainbows turned black and gray.
It's all because an angel on earth
Ascended to heaven.

FOR THE WINNER
(Fable Poetry)

During summer, a squirrel
Finds nuts in a log tunnel.
Some of these are eaten
While most are being hidden.

It never stops working in this fall,
Finding nuts even in a grassy hall.
Every squirrel is doing the same,
Preparing for the winter to tame.

Then north wind blows,
Every snowflake glows.
Foods are lacking.
Air is death, freezing.

Every squirrel has to emerge
Victorious in this winter
Or else they will be submerged
To hardships, life to suffer.

When equinox gives balance,
Life is another chance to dance.
Goodbye to challenging winter
For spring is for the winner.

DESTINY
(Fibonacci Poetry)

If
You're
Really
Mine, my love.
Even you leave me,
You will always come back to me
Because I strongly believe in love and destiny.

TRUE LOVE
(Flamenca Poetry)

I believe in true love
That never dies but flies.
Searching the whole world,
For the special flower
Making the heart's room bloom.

True love is just waiting
When time rhymes in chime.
Breeze whispered love songs.
Believe in destiny.
Finally, it has come.

When you find this flower
Hold, do not let it go.
Put sun, cultivate it.
Water with love and care
For love glows when it grows.

True love gives you honey.
Sweetness like tweeting bird
Makes heart sing in joy.
When waiting means true love,
It is worth waiting for.

ABRA KADABRA
(Free Verse)

"Abra kadabra!" with a simple wave of a wand,
Wings of darkness came out, covering my place.
Coldness wrapped my body and thrown to abyss.
My heart was stabbed and started to bleed.

Abra kadabra was the death of my world.
My breath was swirled and life was chaotic.
Without you, my life would be cold and empty.
The days and nights were both dark and tight.

Flowers wilted and rainbows were evenings.
Rain and pain were endless, life was astray.
My world started to crumble, life was unfair.

Seasons continued to roll and from my fall,
A magical voice made a call, "Abra kadabra!"
You appeared when my soul was almost over.

From your heart and your hat, love came out.
Flowers bloomed, rainbows turned bright.
The sun smiled and blue sky appeared.
Warmth and love healed my wounded heart.
Darkness and sadness melted.

I was speechless for I didn't expect you.
The one I was waiting, didn't return
But you rescued me in this tragic.
Love is magic that's hard to explain.

Your hat is your heart where doves came out.
Heralds of peace and love, you're my true joy.
And now, as I wear my best smile
While waiting you here at this fated altar,
I humbly thanked the greatest Magician
As you walked down this destined aisle.

WARM LOVE IN WINTER
(Free Verse

There are times
When life is winter.
The once warm life
Turns to freezing death.

Everywhere you see,
The ground, the trees
Are icy paintings
Of being lifeless.

The one you hear,
The whisper of the wind
Is a snowy serenade
Of birds' requiem.

You can also taste
The bitter kiss of snowflakes
And frosted air enters your lungs
Almost freezing your heart.

But I want you to remember,
You are always in my heart.
Even at your worst winter,
My love will never get cold.

PEACE AND SILENCE
(Golden Shovel) and (Shape Poetry)

I know where my life and dreams would go.

Be at peace with the people, live placidly.

Challenges, dead ends even in its amid,

Life is not easy but always trust the

Lord. Avoid people who love noise

For they disturb your inner peace and

Control your busy life, avoid all these haste.

Have time for yourself, for your love ones and

Love more, give more to dear to you, remember

That happiness is just in your heart, no matter what

The world may throw stones at. you, still be at peace.

Always smile at people, be grateful and look up there.

Hear your inner voice and songs of love that may

Remind you to always follow your heart and be

At peace always where ever you are in.

Our souls need peace and silence.

After Max Ehrmann "Desiderata" (1ˢᵗ stanza, 1ˢᵗ line- Go placidly amid the noise and haste, and remember what peace there maybe in silence.)

IN HARMONY
(Haiku Sonnet)

Colors are bright light.
Painting the world full of smiles
Gives birth to beauty.

Colors are music
Melodious songs of nature
Rhythm of the heart.

Red, blue, green, yellow
Whatever color it is
Tastes like honey.

They are like flowers.
Each hue gives unique sweet-scent
Smell of paradise.

Colors live in harmony.
Learn to use all the colors.

BLESSING IN DISGUISE
(Idiomatic Poetry)

Out of hand, I had no clue.
A perfect storm raged so loud.
Then suddenly, a bolt from the blue,
I turned useless, helpless under a cloud.

People turned a deaf ear.
They left me out in cold,
Shut their eyes when I came near
And burned bridges, nothing to hold.

Faced the storm under the weather.
You came as a blessing in disguise.
Rescued me and got your act together.
You came as right as rain, what a surprise!

You showed me the other side of the coin.
Handled me with kid gloves, love you gave
Moved heaven and earth for we to rejoin
Until I was on the crest of a wave.

Thanks, I hit the jackpot.
As I strike while the iron is hot.
Happy, I'm on top of the world.
Blessed I am, as good as gold.

RAIN
(Imayo Poetry)

I looked up in the dark sky- life storm is coming.
Rain descended from heaven- blessings in disguise.
Endured till I learned to smile- the rhythm of rain.
The sound and the smell of rain- are smiling angels.

SOMEWHERE
(Interlocking Rubaiyat)

I want to travel to a certain place,
To give myself a peaceful breathing space,
To rest my tired soul from endless hard rain,
And to enjoy the place known for its grace.

This place called somewhere unlocks me from chain,
Sets me free, making me king of this plain,
Reach for my dream, touching the clear blue sky,
Gives me the wings, freedom is what I gain.

This somewhere, streams will no longer run dry.
Birds can fly high, my dreams will never die.
Days and nights, both filled with smiles and flowers
Sun, moon and stars will never say goodbye.

I love this somewhere, sweets never get sour.
Clouds and leaves are angels of love showers.
Breeze listens to the beatings of my heart.
How I wish I'd stay there in endless hours.

THE MOST RADIATING BEAUTY
(Irregular Ode)

Deep down in the earth crust,
Far from the bliss of paradise,
Lies an ordinary mineral of pure dirt,
Facing its tribulation for it to convert.

It suffered continuous hardships.
Pain and challenges are the whips.
Refined by extreme temperature
And hammered by high pressure.

Time came when the pure dirt
Transformed, no longer to be hurt.
Possessing the radiating beauty
That even fairies couldn't display.

When the volcano got angry,
This beauty danced gracefully.
Rhythmically flowed with this chance,
Grabbing this eruption to advance.

When it reached the ground,
All life forms are drowned.
Because this beautiful creation,
Became everyone's inspiration.

You're the most radiating beauty of this world.
You're the clearest, possessing the heart of gold.
Your will is indestructible from any challenges,
And your soul is flawless, free from any malice.

You are the diamond of my life.
Your beauty dominates all the strife,
Making other gems to dream in wonder.
This diamond, she's my radiating mother.

THE SELFLESS FIRE
(Irregular Ode)

Teachers are fire of the modern world.
They keep on shining for the learners to learn.
They brighten the potentials of these children
And selflessly shining for everyone's future.

Teachers are fire, protecting their learners from coldness.
There are learners who are neglected and unloved.
Learners who are abandoned and orphaned,
And who crave for warmth and compassion.

Teachers are fire, protecting their learners from darkness.
They can easily give the learning needs of these children
And teachers act beyond their teaching roles.
They act as protectors of molested and abused angels.

Teachers are fire, selflessly shining in the dark
Their fire courageously faces the challenges of the world.
Even against strong wind and rain, their fire is inextinguishable.
Their fire provides light in the darkest night.

Teachers are fire, shining and warming not only the children in the school
But also to those people who haven't set foot on this learning ground.
Children who are forced to work, old people who are struck by poverty-
They are also learners who are dearly served by these teachers.

Teachers are fire, selflessly serving not only the school
But the entire community where they belong.
Their fire is enough to affect a nation or the whole world
Because their legacy is etched in everyone's heart.

Illustrated by Jema Elizabeth A. Cejero

SUNSET
(Irregular Ode)

Sunset is the goddess of autumn colors
Who loves to kiss the peaceful horizon.
It loves wearing cottons of tangerine,
Gold, ruby and other sparkling lights.

Sunset is the best painter of the sky.
Her artwork is reflected in a calm sea
Where fishes are gracefully dancing
While the sea waves create music.

Fairies offer their sweetest songs
To glorify the lady of autumn colors.
Her last beam gives hope to the land
By showing her last smile of the day.

She is the giver of soothing darkness.
To give your tired soul a time to rest
And when you're ready for the next day,
She would smile at you to wake you up.

MY MISTRESS
(Kyrielle)

In the past, hunger was my day.
Struggled to have food was my way.
My life was roaming in distress
Until I was found by mistress.

My night before was dark and cold.
Sadness was a sight to behold.
My life as a cat, full of stress
Until I was found by mistress.

She's the only fire in my heart.
Her true love is the magic art.
Night is moonless, sad enchantress
Until I was found by mistress.

Her fire is becoming dimmer.
My mistress, I am losing her.
World is crumbling, my strong fortress
Until I was found by mistress.

PARADISE
(Kyrielle Sonnet)

This world is a true paradise.
It gives me wisdom, makes me wise.
It gives each word a life and look.
Full of magic, this place called book.

I turned its pages and I saw
A huge phoenix with golden claws,
Singing, playing to a small rook.
Full of magic, this place called book.

I saw a lot in this journey,
Traveled through time of destiny.
I gained wisdom, flowed like a brook.
Full of magic, this place called book.

This world is a true paradise.
Full of magic, this place called book.

WIELDING A SHARP BLADE
(Lannet)

A tongue has blade sharper than a dagger.
It couldn't make one bleed physically
But it could directly pierce through the heart
And break one's peaceful life to smithereens.

A person whose life wounded by this tongue
Might lose hope in life refusing to shine
For this poor soul believes in what he hears.
Words uttered are blades with too much power.

Use tongue to tell the beauty of the world.
Be generous to give praises and love.
Express words to make friends and create peace.
Never use its blade to hurt and to slay.

Like a blade, a tongue should be used with care.
Wield its sharp blade to make a better world.

OUR OLD DAYS
(La'Tuin)

Sitting alone in this loneliness,
I started thinking our old days.
Can't help myself but to cry in pain
Felt bitter in this emptiness.

To be with you is my happiness.
You are my true colorful rays.
You are the rainbow in every rain.
You drive away all my sadness.

Dear, I only need your forgiveness.
It's my fault and I'll find all ways
Just for you to love me again.
With you, life is full of sweetness.

Sitting alone in this loneliness,
I started thinking our old days
Can't help myself but to cry in pain
Felt bitter in this emptiness.

PLAYING CHESS
(Lento)

Think of a plan when playing chess.

Ink your mind with a plan to advance.

Sync all the movements of your pieces.

Shrink your opponent to give no chance.

Be careful every time you move a piece.

See to it that your king is secured.

Free your moves from every blunder.

Glee is felt when playmate is lured.

JUST A CLOUD
(Lethrannaegecht Mor Poetry)

The sky is my home.
I can block the sun
When it is too hot
And not just for fun.

In me is water
That the land wanted.
I make life to beat
For those sweet-hearted.

The canvas up high
Shows cottons of fall.
I paint varied shapes
Like trees, apes and wall.

I am just a cloud
Drifting in this space.
Giving your sunset
A net in full grace.

MY FRIEND
(Limerick Poetry)

I have a friend claiming he's like a bird.
He's a good singer, that's his word.
But when he sings,
Life has no more swing.
His voice is a crying hawk, so weird.

DAYS OF THE WEEK
(List Poetry)

This afternoon,
Sunday, the tycoon
Monday, the racoon
Saw Tuesday in a cocoon,
And Wednesday holding a spoon.
They rode on Thursday, a balloon,
Owned by Friday, a monsoon
With Saturday going to the moon.

DANDELIONS
(Luc Bat Poetry)

When dandelions bloom
From a bed full of gloom, wishes
Are born and black ashes
Are doomed by the crashes of light.
Dandelions are bright
Bringing hope in a night of pain.
Dandelions contain
Lessons in life where rain is not
A hindrance but a shot
For them to kiss the spot in glow.
They never stop to go
From any blow, to show to all
Not to quit, stop or fall
But to fight and grow tall in glee.
Dandelions carry
The wishes as they're free to fly,
Waving their sweet goodbye
To touch and kiss the sky of hope.

THE BIRD
(Madrigal Poetry)

Bird flies up to the sky, flying so high.
Wind blows, sun glows, the bird feeling so low
But still, flaps wings so hard, dreams to pursue.

All trees cheered up the bird, flowers said, "Hi"
Convinced the bird to tweet, to smile, to go.
Bird flies up to the sky, flying so high.
Wind blows, sun glows, the bird feeling so low.

Bird spreads its wings, ready to try and fly.
Powered by its desire, follow the flow
Pursue its dream is what it needs to do.
Bird flies up to the sky, flying so high.
Wind blows, sun glows, the bird feeling so low
But still, flaps wings so hard, dreams to pursue.

FINISH LINE
(Magic 9 Poetry)

Life is full of ups, downs and curved roads,
A race for the finish line but not a competition.
Some are slow or have stopped cos of heavy load.
Others are fast, their road is smooth and clear.
Some roads are narrow, others are broad.
Patience and persistence should be their fuel.
Sometimes, detour is needed, destiny needs to decode.
Always take a step closer to destination, a mission.
Soon finish line is inches away, joy overflowed.

COUNT YOUR BLESSINGS
(Masnavi Poetry)

When the sky turns dark, life has no more spark.
Flowers stopped to bloom, sadness is the doom.
Nothing's left but hope, you go to that slope.
Climb the highest peak, do not feel so weak.
Have faith, start climbing with perfect timing.
When you reach the top, take a rest and stop.
See the sights around, hear the sweetest sound.
Smell the green grasses, scent of fresh gases.
Taste the peace of mind, eyes no longer blind.
Ears are set to hear, songs of care turn clear.
You are still lucky, you hold the true key.
The fakes have left you, those snakes let them go.
You're left of few friends whom you can depend.
True love warms your heart but ne'er been apart.
A home full of love, a gift from above.
You think you're the worst, truly the reversed.
You're terribly great with some shining traits.
Always face your pain, rain will not remain.
Wear smile, be happy and set yourself free.
Look at the bright side as you take your stride.
Joys are everywhere, you can find it here.
Count all your blessings, flap your wings and
sing.

THE LIGHT
(Mini-monoverse)

Friends are gold
Hands to hold
When it's cold
Stays till old
Never scold

In your night
Time to fight
In this tight
Friends are light
Make life bright

THE ARMS
(Modern Pastoral Poetry)

Today's battle is about to end
And time for my soul to mend.
My body worked the whole day
To harvest blessings in bouquet.

As the wings of the night started to creep,
Sadness in my heart submerged in the deep.
I peacefully watched the magnificent sky.
Cottons of gold and tangerine float high.

The birds are fairies of pure joy
As they fly high, invading to deploy.
The tiredness and sadness in my heart
Are dispersed in the air and began to part.

The sea is the mirror of the sky,
Showing its beauty to a passerby.
Sending its waves to the shores
Creating melodious music as it roars.

I sat on the shore and closed my eyes
To offer a prayer to my Greatest Ally
His smiles and love are in this place.
The dusk, the sea and the sky, I can see His face.

The birds are singing their best goodnight.
The cold grains of sand are stars bringing light.
The breeze made the sound of the leaves rustling.
The island is my heart where it keeps on beating.

This dusk is the arms of Almighty
He treated me as His precious baby.
Because tonight, His embracing soothing darkness
Promises a new day that will fill my emptiness.

LISTEN IN SILENCE
(Monologue)

Do you have a friend who seems so strong,
Whom you've never seen him complaining
About life, his relationships and everything?
He is like a sun with so much brightness
Or a moon that never leave you at night.
A friend whose ears are ready to listen
And seems to be always smiling and okay.
This kind of friend, you need to take care.
Don't ever believe of what you're seeing.
Maybe this friend is battling a silent war.
Have time also to listen at his silence.
Don't ever mistake that his calmness
Is always a sea of tranquility and peace.
There are times that you need to stop
Sharing all your pain and negativities.
Stop asking his time just to bombard him
With all your problems and frustrations
Because you just don't know, your friend
Is sailing alone against a sea raging waves
And is silently shouting for care and help.
Now, it's your turn to listen to your friend
Even if he looks okay and prefers silence.

SILVERY MOON
(Monorhyme Poetry)

When mighty sun began to hide,
The moon o'er the hill was untied.
It danced, took the clouds as its ride
And the twinkling stars by its side
Were kind fairies that loved to slide.
Its wings of silvery light dyed
The gloomy shadows of misguide
And desert of sadness was dried.
Seas rejoiced with its foaming tide.
Happiness refused to subside.
Glowing fireflies started to glide.
Silvery light kiss was supplied.
Darkness and loneliness both cried
And my devils were terrified.
The ghostly fear that I defied
Was all gone in this peaceful wide.
Beacon of hope that once denied
And love in me that almost died
Were like phoenix, freed from its tied.
Silvery moon, thanks for your guide.

UNITY IN DIVERSITY
(Monotetra Poetry)

Unity in diversity
Is a challenge from Almighty.
Through this, we all become mighty,
Love unity, love unity.

Even the fish that swim have rule.
To beat their foes, they formed a school.
Enemies are made like a fool.
Fish are so cool, fish are so cool.

Small streams worked as one for the sea.
They never get tired like a bee.
They fill up the sea, love to see.
Sea not empty, sea not empty.

During sunset clouds work as one.
Each shows its hue, joining the fun,
Working together for the sun
A day is done, a day is done.

Let us take lessons from nature
Gives us wisdom and not to lure.
Diversity makes life so pure
I am so sure, I am so sure.

MY CHILD, MY FLOWER
(Multiple Haiku)

My dear little child,
I'm your most caring angel
Offering my love.

My fluttering wings
Covering you at all times
Giving you true love.

First rays of sunlight,
Make your petals beautiful.
Accept the warm love.

You may not see me
When you open your petals
For my life is gone.

Please listen to me,
Beautiful flower of love.
Grow with elegance.

Always wear your smile,
Expressing the excitement
Of joy and laughter.

Grow beautifully.
You're the fairy of nature,
Flower of sweetness.

Dance under the sun,
Sway gracefully with the wind.
Keys to happy life.

This is my last kiss.
My dear beloved flower.
My dear little child.

THE URN
(Narrative Poetry)

In the outskirts of a city,
A place for a trash like me,
Stood my thatched house-
Living here with my spouse.

Uncountable years spent in this place.
It was poor, noisy and dirty space.
Causing my wife to be sickly
But I still love her dearly.

We earned money by selling anything.
It was a very hard means of living.
We need to roll our money,
Or else we would die like nobody.

Then, COVID-19 hit the world,
Creating problems, future is blurred.
Making the poor to be poorer,
The hungry to be hungrier.

The city was locked down,
No money, no food to be found.
What should I do?
Going out is taboo.

My wife was sick as dog.
Handled her with kid gloves.
Health was becoming worse.
It was like living in a curse.

Days flowed roughly
And I diced with death.
Have to plan clearly
Or else she would lose her breath.

Reported the condition of my wife
And rescue was done promptly.
Brought to hospital to save her life
While I was put in a room, lonely.

I felt fear and helpless.
I felt like hopeless.
Wanted to stay with beloved
But it was not allowed.

My wife is my everything
And I'm also her everything.
We only have a simple dream-
To live together in gleam.

Time sadly flowed in my solace.
Tears flooded my sealed place.
I missed my wife so badly.
Wondering if she was treated nicely.

A new gloomy day came
And someone knocked the door.
He was carrying an urn
And my world stopped!

Heaven started to dim.
Clouds were crying.
Birds sang the requiem.
My heart was deadly in pain.

My life lost its rainbow colors.
The future showed black doors.
Regretted for not seeing her,
And caring her in her last hour.

After the quarantine, I went home.
Saw her face in every part of the house.
This place, full of her memories.
Couldn't stop but to cry my eyes out.

One evening while holding the urn,
A familiar voice was calling my name.
She's dead but I terribly missed her,
Embracing her would ease my pain.

I opened the door and I was frightened.
I saw the familiar face in full vitality,
Asking, "Andres, why are you hugging that urn?"
I felt so happy seeing her blowing a fuse.

ROOTS
(Nonet Poetry)

Children are like branches of a tree.

They grow in their own directions

To bear their flowers and fruits.

Some branches are too low.

Others, extreme high.

But still, they share

The same tree,

Trunk and

Roots.

MORNING BLESSINGS
(Ottava Rima)

Every morning kiss is a great blessing.
The first ray of the sun caressing you
Is a great feeling that makes your heart sing.
You can still see the blue sky and its view
Where birds are flying, spring and hope they bring.
Sunrise is sweet just like this morning dew.
The warmth of the sun melts your heart in joy.
Morning is a blessing, life to enjoy.

Morn is a gift, smile with a grateful heart.
Always listen to the songs of pure love.
See those flowers whose glows ne'er to depart.
Morning is a warm greeting from Above.
The sweetest angel for the day to start
That showers blessings in the wings of dove.
Thank God and always wear your smile today.
It's the best way to embrace this new day.

BOOMERANG
(Palindrome Poetry)

Life involves karma.
Kindness produces smile
Positivity makes day brighter.
Always help people
For angels are miracles.
Kindness and positivity
"boomerang"
Positivity and kindness.
Miracles are angels for
People help always.
Brighter day makes positivity.
Smile produces kindness.
Karma involves life.

PARADE OF COLORS
(Pantoum Poetry)

Parade of bright colors, what a worthy sight!
Red fights for love, the power in full intensity.
Orange has the mighty sunset of autumn light.
Yellow shines the joy and delight of positivity.

Red fights for love, the power in full intensity.
Green is spring of hope, a sight in a mountain.
Yellow shines the joy and delight of positivity.
Blue, the sky and water of peace in a fountain.

Green is spring of hope, a sight in a mountain.
Indigo sings order and integrity full of beauty.
Blue, the sky and water of peace in a fountain.
Violet is a royalty of modesty and spirituality.

Indigo sings order and integrity full of beauty.
Orange has the mighty sunset of autumn light.
Violet is a royalty of modesty and spirituality.
Parade of bright colors, what a worthy sight!

GUAVA
(Pleiades)

Green fruits hanging freely

Greeting with their sweetness

Glowing with their green skin

Growing to offer food

Giving smiles to faunas

Gifts to birds, bats and you

Great are these sweet-scent fruits

FIRST DAY IN TEACHING
(Prose Poetry)

Every experience that is done for the first time is usually a memorable and holds meaning in our lives. This first experience might be our first crush, our first time of swimming in a river or even our first kiss to our special someone. One of my first-time experiences is my first day in teaching. My first day of teaching holds a special spot in my heart. For me, it is a treasure that is worth remembering. This memory still makes my heart sing with joy. My first day of teaching was in a private school, somewhere in the City of San Fernando, La Union, Philippines way back 2002.

On that first day, I felt so excited and nervous. I was excited because I could finally apply what I have learned in college and it was also the realization of my dream. I was nervous because I was afraid that I might not be a good teacher. These were my feelings on that day but still I wore my best smile and needed to calm myself. I imagined myself like I was walking in a garden. Upon entering the school and my classroom, I saw different kinds of plants possessing unique beauty and elegance. Each of this plant was beautiful on its own way and none was considered ugly nor bad. Some plants had already few flowers but none yet had fruits, others were still blooming and few were still in buds. These plants were still young and they need care for them to totally flourish and blossom.

These plants had different needs. Some of these plants needed direct sunlight while others grew under the shade. Some needed abundant water to grow while others did not. These plants were my learners who had different learning styles and different learning needs and who had their own pace in development but still, all of them were uniquely beautiful, skilled, talented and important.

My first day in teaching was full of life, smiles and positivity. I was the gardener cultivating these plants for them to totally flourish and blossom. These learners, I water them with wisdom. Just like the sun, I offered them my warm compassion and my light was a guide for them to discover, improve or enhance their strengths, skills and talents. The teachers and school offered a strong and rich foundation for all the learners just like a plant planted in a fertile soil. The garden was my classroom and the school while the plants were my learners.

Illustrated by: Jema Elizabeth A. Cejero

TREES AND BOOKS
(Quatern Poetry)

Like trees, books love light and bear golds.
Through light, the pages of a book
And leaves of a tree turn useful.
Leaves are for trees, pages for books.

Trees act likc books and work the same.
Like trees, books love light and bear golds.
Light is needed to feel the soul
Of each word contained in a leaf.

Through light, trees bear fruits that are golds
While books give the fruits of wisdom.
Like trees, books love light and bear golds.
These fruits are for body and mind.

Trees love to reach the sky above
And books provide chances and hope
Making every dream to come true.
Like trees, books love light and bear golds.

TRICKY LIFE
(Reverse Poetry Form)

Life is always singing and dancing
So you'll never hear me say that
Life is all about sorrow and pain.
It is true to say that
My life is full of meaning and joy.
And this is not true for me-
My life is always a disaster.
I always believe that
I exist to love and be loved.
And I don't believe that
My existence is for loneliness.
This one is true about me-
Life has always been kind to me.
I refuse to believe that
Life is unfair and injustice.
For I know deep in my heart that
Life is all about love and smiles.
There is no way that
Life will get wrong.

(Now read from bottom to top)

Life will get wrong.
There is no way that
Life is all about love and smiles.
For I know...

SHADOWS IN THE NIGHT
(Rictameter)

Be still.
Amidst the trees,
Souls are silent tonight.
Be watchful of your surroundings.
Ignore those shadows trying to lure you.
Demons are plotting to snatch you.
Remain awake tonight.
Be vigilant.
Be still.

Illustrated by: Jema Elizabeth A. Cejero

LUNAR HALO
(Riddle Poetry)

Appear when storm embraces the sky
While the queen of the night
Elegantly hanging in the sky.
Seven different colors of fairy might,
Circling the queen in the sky!

EFFECTIVE PARENTING
(Rispetto)

Children are all angels sent down from above
While parents receive them as their greatest gifts.
These children are all precious gems who need love.
Teach them to stand up on their own and give lifts
To any pressure they'll face with peace like doves.
Children have to be trained to cross any rift.
They can do these if parents are good enough
In training up their kids- parenting is tough.

These kids, treat them with so much respect and fair.
Teach them to be kind, just and being grateful.
Enhance all their potentials, never compare
For every child is a gift and beautiful.
Give joy to your kids, give your time, love to share
And always make them feel that they are wonderful.
Live what you preach for kids believe what they see.
And most of all, put God in your family.

THE PENCIL
(Rondeau Poetry)

Like a pencil, life needs a Guiding Hand.
A pencil always follows the command
And never try to disobey its guide.
This life has a Guiding Hand in his side.
Life is like a pencil to understand.

A pencil faced pressure to make a brand,
Needs to be sharpened for it to expand.
Its writings and life need to coincide.
Like a pencil...

A pencil is like footprints in the sand.
Uses its core to leave marks that are grand.
Life has heart which he could use to preside.
Only allow the good things to reside.
Life when gone, his writing marks stay to stand.
Like a pencil...

HORIZON
(Sedoka Poetry)

I'm just wondering
Why is there a horizon
That's impossible to reach?

The sea and the sky,
Destiny set them apart
But horizon made them kiss.

Illustrated by: Jema Elizabeth A. Cejero

SHOOTING STAR
(Septolet Poetry)

Dark sky,
Watching stars,
Waiting.

Suddenly,
Streak of light
So beautiful,
Make a wish.

WILTED FLOWERS
(Shakespearean Sonnet)

Our love was like flowers that were blooming,
Full of honey, so sweet felt like heaven.
Our hearts were both warmly beating, booming,
Sweet-scent swaying with the breeze in haven

Out of nowhere, flowers wilted and died.
Your love turned cold, your heart refused to beat.
Rivers stopped from flowing and seas were dried.
You left my world, never shall be complete.

Years passed but this feeling remained the same.
I love no one but you, that was not strange.
My love was still burning, kept me aflame.
Never to be burned out, my love won't change.

Wilted flowers offered on your white tomb
Were my crushed heart beating with love in gloom.

THE DYING CANDLE
(Shape Poetry)

Time
Limits me
To live for more,
Spend my life with you.
I love you so much, my dear child.
I only want to continue living with you
To bring you the light for you to be guided
For you to have a brighter and happier future.
I am a candle whose wax was almost used up.
Want to burn more so I can give you light.
Sorry my child, if my light is limited.
I can no longer shine your path.
Just promise me my child.
Always love yourself.
Be brave enough.
Live!

KEEP ON GLOWING
(Soliloquy)

Tonight, the moon was shining alone
For all the stars were covered by clouds.
Moonbeam seemed to be embracing me.
I lied on grasses, facing the dark sky.
Saw the moon and gave my bitter smile.
Deep feelings started to stab me again.
My life has always been in storms.
I don't know when these storms will end.
I lost my dreams, hope and confidence.
What else should I lose? My sanity?
I have already cried the blood tears.
But why my life has been like this?
People I helped and cared, they left me.
Life indeed is unfair and treacherous.
But this moon, its beam is caressing me.
Its cold light filled up my emptiness.
This moon keeps on changing, glowing.
It never stops from waxing and waning.
It always rises to beat this darkest night.
Yes, I should be the moon shining bright
That never surrender against this dark.
I should always rise and show my light.
I'll keep on glowing and let my radiance
Beat the darkness and bring me to success.
Let my light glow happiness and love.

KING AND QUEEN
(Somonka Poetry)

Oh! Queen of my heart,
You're the angel of my life.
The first time we met
Was the time I saw true love.
My heart beats only for you.

Your words touch my heart
Oh, my sweet beloved king!
Your touch and your kiss
Are love so strong but gentle.
Promise me, don't break my heart.

MY BUTTERFLY
(Song Poetry)

I remember the day when you were born.
It was the day when mama's life was thorn.
Heaven had cried, pain was beyond terrible.
Life shambled and it was a merciless gamble.

My dearest baby, you are my butterfly.
You are the bright light in my darkest sky
And the garden rainbow smiling up high.

My butterfly, this is my promise to you.
I'll do anything just for you, this is true.
I'm always your supporter- your wings
And your wind guiding you in spring.

My butterfly, you give colors into my life.
Your presence simply puts away my strife.
The queen of our life whom we extremely miss
As she watches us from heaven is surely in bliss.

My dearest baby, you are my butterfly.
You are the bright light in my darkest sky
And the garden rainbow smiling up high.

My dearest baby, you are my butterfly.
You are the bright light in my darkest sky
And the garden rainbow smiling up high.

TRUE BEAUTY
(Stornello Poetry)

True beauty is not all about looks and face
But it is all about in your heart and grace.
It's all about showing kindness in this space.

True beauty adds positivity and smiles.
It grows with the passing years, a shining style.
It never hurt but gives light in every mile.

RAINBOW
(Tanka Poetry)

To see a rainbow
That appears after the rain.
You need to endure
Life's storms no matter how strong.
Fight and never surrender.

SUMMER SPEAKS
(Tautogram)

Shadows seemed strong,
Scaring simple soul.
Scheming sharp strategies,
Stealing someone's spot.

Sun struggled,
Showered sunshine.
Shocking sinful shadows,
Sorrows stopped.

Sweetness sprouted.
Sunflowers smiled,
Singing songs sweetly.
Summer speaks success.

OLD HAPPY DAYS
(Terzanelle)

I'm starting to miss my old happy days.
How I wish this cursed pandemic would end.
Longing to bath from the abundant rays.

I can't even visit my closest friend.
I missed granny so much and all the fun.
How I wish this cursed pandemic would end.

During vacation, I felt I have won.
We used to visit granny in the farm.
I missed granny so much and all the fun.

In this break, summer season gave much charm.
Cousins brought me to exciting places.
We used to visit granny in the farm.

We climbed up the hills, saw nature faces
Like rivers, falls, forests and many more.
Cousins brought me to exciting places.

But now, we're locked up, not allowed to explore.
I'm starting to miss my old happy days.
Like rivers, falls, forests and many more.
Longing to bath from the abundant rays.

THE TWISTER AND THE TWINKLER
(Tongue Twister Poetry)

A twister twisting to crack a twisted twinkler

But the twinkler twisted back the twister.

The twister and the twinkler tweeted plaque

Twisting, twirling like teasing twins in black.

They twiddled in tweeter to quack and to tweet

But both were track by a twisted twirling twit.

The twisted twirling twit twitched and locked

The twister and the twinkler in a twitching sack.

LAST
(Trian Rannaigechta Moire Poetry)

Last is our song
Where birds can sing
Of nature's sound
Spring, sing and swing.

When flowers bloom,
Life seemed to bless.
Breeze of joy blows.
Lovers feel bliss.

Fear let it go
For love to glow.
Heart feels so great.
The love will grow.

Heart when in love
Is not all lust.
Seeing the light,
The love will last.

EACH MOMENT
(Trianglet)

Time

Is bright.

Live with sense.

Smile each moment.

Plant seeds of kindness.

Bear fruits of greatness.

Dance life problems.

Don't be tensed

Of night

Time.

A LEAF
(Tricube Poetry)

A leaf sprouts
New life starts
Bringing hope

Light showers
Nature sings
Life at peak

Days, nights rolled
Leaf got old
Turning gold

GOLDEN HEARTS
(Trimeric Poetry)

In this journey, you simply have a choice.

You may pick trashes or focus on the goal.

You live in spring of hope or winter of lesson.

Above all, keep those with golden hearts.

You may pick trashes or focus on the goal.

Trashes are trashes, why should you pick?

Focus on your dream, reach for your stars.

You live in spring of hope or autumn of colors.

Decide whom you want to be with in summer

And be careful in winter and take its lesson.

Above all, keep those with golden hearts.

They shine without taking your own light

And they even help you to brighten your path.

TOO PAINFUL
(Triolet)

My heart's shattered, light is no more.

Flowers have dried, rainbows are black.

Can't stop my clouds to weep, to pour.

My heart's shattered, light is no more.

My soul wanted to scream, to roar.

You're always here, please do come back.

My heart's shattered, light is no more.

Flowers have dried, rainbows are black.

IN THE DARK
(Tyburn Poetry)

Afraid

Dismayed

Invade

Degrade

I'm afraid and dismayed of this spark,

Hope to invade and degrade this dark.

THE MOUNTAIN
(Vers Beaucoup Poetry)

In this mountain, rain is like a fountain.
Train to sing and dive in a deep spring.
Swing in joy and always follow the flow.
Don't be slow but be fast, have a blast.

This place, the face of nature full of grace.
Embrace the light and always enjoy the sight.
Stop the fight, give your best smile for a while.
End your trial, be free from stress and distress.

Blend with this friend that you can depend.
Spend time and always make a rhyme
As chime of sweet music heals the sick.
Pick a flower, feel its healing power.

DAY AND NIGHT
(Villanelle Poetry)

Day rules my heart, screams my soul sway
Then sunset comes and the moon waves.
Night hugs my heart, pain goes away.

Morning sun strengthens me today
With its light and warmth, here to save.
Day rules my heart, screams my soul sway.

White-gold moon gives soft and cold rays
Soothing my tired soul, shines my cave.
Night hugs my heart, pain goes away.

Sunshine smiles, sun showing my way.
Flowers bloom, warm love has engraved.
Day rules my heart, screams my soul sway.

Moonbeams knock my heart, love to say.
Heals my deep wound, it shines to save.
Night hugs my heart, pain goes away.

Sunshine showers, love smiles today.
Moonbeam knocks, night is to be brave.
Day rules my heart, screams my soul sway.
Night hugs my heart, pain goes away.

VIRTUAL FRIEND
(Zejel Poetry)

We once met in an online game.
We both had the same burning flame
Making us knew each other's name.

We became friends and there was joy
As our soldiers made to deploy,
Invading kingdoms to destroy.
Our names hit the top, so much fame.

Other players joined our success.
There was so much fun, free from stress.
We made plans to keep our progress,
No more sound sleep just for this game.

Till you left without any word,
My virtual world became too blurred.
My virtual friend, longed to be heard.
Miss my friend, hope he feels the same.

THANK YOU
(Double Acrostic Poetry)

(T)his hour, this very momen(T)
(H)appy you're about to finis(H)
(A)ppreciating my poetry Ide(A)
(N)ew poetry forms have bee(N)
(K)nitted to your poetry ban(K)

(Y)ou gave time reading m(Y)
(O)nly authored book. I'm s(O)
(U)ndeniably grateful to yo(U)

ABOUT THE AUTHOR

Jeffrey Dacanay Cejero was born on September 5, 1980, in San Fernando City, La Union, Philippines. His parents are Mr. Arsenio Ramos Cejero, Sr. and Mrs. Felicitas Dacanay-Cejero. He is the youngest child among the seven children. His siblings are Ana Fe, Digna, Estelita, Francis, Nilo, and Junjun who at present have their own families. His family has maintained a strong bond which is a typical characteristic of a Filipino family.

He is married to Maritess Abellera-Cejero. They are gifted with 3 children namely Jema Elizabeth, Mark Wissam, and Catherine Anne. Jeffrey and his wife are both master teachers in public elementary school. They are both teaching in Sison District, Pangasinan, Philippines.

The author is a multigrade teacher at Bila Elementary School. This school is classified as a last mile school in the Philippines. The author has been teaching for 20 years and the 10 years of that was served as a multigrade teacher. A multigrade teacher handles 2 or more classes in one classroom. At present, he is the adviser of grades 5 and 6.

His experiences in multigrade teaching paved the way for him to be a multigrade scholar of the Department of Education where he was sent to University of the Philippines- Diliman Campus to study. He has also received certificates of recognition for being one of the national writers of learning resources for multigrade teaching.

The author loves nature. The author and his family live in a rural place near a range of mountains. The place is surrounded by nature where it is possible to hear the singing of various birds, witness the glowing fireflies at night, and see one of the rarest animals in the world, the endangered species flying lizards. A lot of the author's poems are conceptualized by observing his surroundings.

www.ingramcontent.com/pod-product-compliance
Lightning Source LLC
LaVergne TN
LVHW010530200726
843506LV00013B/2781

9 786214 701384